THE FAITH

THE FAITH
A JOURNEY WITH GOD

DFD 2.3 a study of why to believe

*A NavPress resource published in alliance
with Tyndale House Publishers, Inc.*

NAVPRESSO

NavPress is the publishing ministry of The Navigators, an international Christian organization and leader in personal spiritual development. NavPress is committed to helping people grow spiritually and enjoy lives of meaning and hope through personal and group resources that are biblically rooted, culturally relevant, and highly practical.

For more information, visit www.NavPress.com.

The Faith: A Journey with God DFD 2.3

Copyright © 2004 by The Navigators. All rights reserved.

A NavPress resource published in alliance with Tyndale House Publishers, Inc.

NAVPRESS and the NAVPRESS logo are registered trademarks of NavPress, The Navigators, Colorado Springs, CO. *TYNDALE* is a registered trademark of Tyndale House Publishers, Inc. Absence of ® in connection with marks of NavPress or other parties does not indicate an absence of registration of those marks.

ISBN 978-1-57683-638-5

Cover design by BURNKIT
Creative Team: Eric Johnson, Gabe Filkey, Rachelle Gardner, Kathy Mosier, Pat Reinheimer

Scripture taken from the Holy Bible, *New International Version*,® *NIV*.® Copyright © 1973, 1978, 1984, 2011 by Biblica, Inc.® Used by permission. All rights reserved worldwide.

INTRODUCTION

THE LOGIC OF FAITH

There's a difference between logic and Faith. Logic wants things to be neat and tidy. Logic wants to know that if A is true, then B must always be true. Logic wants to play it safe by renting the Volvo with GPS because it's always well protected and knows where it's going. The problem is, Faith doesn't work like this.

Faith is messier. It requires a level of certainty in the face of absolute uncertainty. Faith takes a giant leap when everything in us screams to stand still. Faith, by definition, implies that there might well be a very logical reason *to be unsure*. If there wasn't, we wouldn't need Faith. The Bible says, "Faith is being sure of what we hope for and certain of what we do not see" (Hebrews 11:1).

Following God—giving your whole life to Him—isn't merely a cognitive, logical decision you make. It can start like that, but it never ends there because giving your life to Christ isn't always logical. There's a lot of "foolishness" involved. Often, it isn't the safe thing to do. Just look at the recklessness of the Cross.

It all starts to make sense when you read 1 Corinthians 1:18-31. (You might want to take a look before starting chapter 1.) In this passage, Paul grappled with the fact that God's logic simply isn't human logic—it's far greater than we can comprehend. That's why we need Faith. With Faith, we can begin to grasp the profound depths of God's infinite logic—His perfectly messy, paradoxical, beautiful logic.

With that said, without checking our brains at the door, let's look at why we believe what we believe.

CHAPTER 1

THE FATHER

Faith in God is threefold: It's an educated conclusion of your mind; it's a visceral reaction in your heart; and it's a resolute decision to live it out, even in the face of death. Mind, heart, action. All three must be involved in a real and effective Faith.

Faith begins and ends with God. Let's start our study of the Faith by digging a little deeper into who God is. Remember, behind all Faith, the Spirit works in mysterious ways to open our hearts, souls, and minds to the unsurpassable glory and significance of God. Before you start, pray that God will strengthen and grow your Faith in Him.

REVIEW: WHO IS GOD?

1. What are some of God's names? What do they mean to the Faith?

   Genesis 17:1:

   Psalm 95:6:

Luke 11:2:

1 Timothy 6:15:

2. Read Isaiah 45:18-25. From this passage, explain a few things about God's character that can bolster your Faith.

3. What else does the Bible say about God's nature?

Isaiah 40:28:

John 4:24:

4. God is *omniscient, omnipresent, omnipotent, eternal,* and *immutable*. Match the verses below with one of these traits of God (you may need to look them up in a dictionary first). Briefly surmise why each trait is essential to a solid Faith in God.

Psalm 90:2:

Jeremiah 23:24:

Jeremiah 32:17:

James 1:17:

1 John 3:20:

5. How do David's thoughts about God in 1 Chronicles 29:10-13 coincide with or differ from the way you think about God?

6. Using David's prayer as a pattern, write your own prayer to God, praising Him for who He is and acknowledging how Faith in Him has changed your life (if it has).

> Without doubt the mightiest thought the mind can entertain is the thought of God.
>
> —A. W. TOZER*

7. Humans, for all their flaws, hold a unique place and calling within creation. To illustrate this point:

   a. Read and summarize Genesis 1:26-27.

---

*A. W. Tozer, *The Knowledge of the Holy* (New York: Harper and Brothers, 1961), p. 10.

b. Read and summarize 1 Peter 1:15-16.

c. Explain how the fact in the Genesis passage relates to the command in 1 Peter.

8. Major problems arise in our lives when we don't accurately understand who the Father is. For example, if we don't have Faith that God is holy, we won't prioritize holy living in our own lives. If we don't believe God is loving, we won't emphasize true love in our lives. With that in mind, read the following verses. Each contains a truth about God's character. Decipher what each verse says about God and then consider what problems might arise if you didn't accept this attribute of God.

Deuteronomy 7:9:

Psalm 130:3-4:

1 John 1:5:

1 John 4:16:

9. Think back to *The Walk: DFD* 2.2. You learned that God is sovereign—He's in control, even in difficult times. Tell how each verse below affirms the supremacy of God in all circumstances and how this applies to your Faith.

Proverbs 21:1:

Isaiah 14:27:

Acts 4:26-28:

FAITH IN THE FATHER

10. Look up Jeremiah 31:3, John 3:16, and Ephesians 3:19.

    a. Summarize what each passage teaches about God's love.

    b. Why does God's love matter to your Faith?

11. How do we become "children of God" (John 1:12-13; Galatians 3:26)?

12. Why do you think God defines His relationship with us as Father and child? What does it mean to your Faith that God, the Creator and Master, wants to be your Father, your Dad? Write a short paragraph to explain your answer.

13. If God is indeed our Dad, how should we react when He lovingly guides us in the right direction (Hebrews 12:7-10)?

14. Read the first sentence of 2 Chronicles 16:9. From this passage, draw some conclusions about God's heart and His love for those who put their Faith in Him.

15. Next, read Psalm 46:1.

   a. How is the Father described in this passage?

   b. Give a personal example of a time when you experienced this aspect of God's character in your life.

WHAT DOES THE FATHER EXPECT FROM US?

16. What does God want from us? Read closely Psalm 51:16-17. Try to explain in your own words what "a broken spirit" means. Does it mean that God wants us to be sad or depressed?

17. How should we respond to God's call? (Hint: Read Psalm 95:6.)

18. Look up the following verses: Deuteronomy 10:12, Psalm 100:4, and Hebrews 11:6. Use them to write another short paragraph, this time explaining some of the essentials of having a God-honoring Faith.

In all His dealings with us, God works for our good. In prosperity, He tests our gratitude; in mediocrity, our contentment; in misfortune, our submission; and in all things, our obedience and Faith in Him.

19. Using all you've learned so far in the DFD 2.0 series or other studies you've completed, define *worship*. (For a clue, go back to Psalm 95:6.)

20. Why do you think worship is so vital to our Faith?

21. In what ways do you worship and honor God with your life?

22. Read 1 Chronicles 28:9. How does David's advice to his son relate to your life today?

23. What does Psalm 46:10, one more quote from David, teach us about knowing God?

SUMMARY

Review the chapter and write your own summary, answering these three questions:

- Why do you have Faith in God?
- How does God love us?
- What does God expect from us?

CHAPTER 2

BELIEVING IN GOD'S WORD

Imagine that you see someone across a crowded room—someone you think might just be your type. You weave your way through the crowd to the other side of the room. As you get closer, you notice that this person is definitely your type. And then it happens. The mystery person speaks, and it's all over. *I've never met someone so* _____ (boring, stuck-up, shallow) *in my life,* you think to yourself. The relationship is over before it began.

You can't love someone without loving what he or she says. If she's boring or egotistical, if he's arrogant or clueless, you know right away that a relationship isn't possible. In a similar way, you can't love God and not love His Word. Without God's Word, there is no Faith because "faith comes from hearing the message, and the message is heard through the word of Christ" (Romans 10:17). The Bible is God's story and His Law, all in a personal letter to His children.

If we put our Faith in God, we will love His Word because it takes us closer to Him and helps us better understand the perfect love He has for us. Falling in love with God and His Word is central to the Faith.

1. How highly does God think of His Word (Psalm 138:2)?

2. In 2 Timothy 3:14-17, Paul reminded Timothy of the central place of God's Word in our lives. Write down two or three things regarding

God's Word that strike you as interesting or important. Explain how they apply to your Faith.

3. What did other writers of the Bible say? How does each of the following passages reflect the real authorship of the Bible back to God?

Deuteronomy 28:1-2:

2 Samuel 23:1-3:

Jeremiah 1:6-9:

1 Thessalonians 2:13:

THE RELIABILITY OF THE SCRIPTURES

4. Read the following passages. How does each one strengthen your Faith in the reliability of the Word of God?

   Joshua 23:14:

   Psalm 33:4:

   Proverbs 30:5-6:

5. Next, read what Luke said about God's Word in Luke 1:1-4. What conclusion can you draw about putting Faith in the Bible?

6. Skip ahead to 2 Peter 1:15-21. Peter was referring to an event called the Transfiguration that happened while Jesus walked the

earth. (If you're not familiar with it, read about it in Matthew 17, Mark 9, and Luke 9.) Use Peter's statement to answer the following.

   a. Do you think it is important that Peter and others were eyewitnesses? Why or why not (verses 16-18)?

   b. What else did Peter mention as a major confirmation of the validity of God's Word (verse 19)?

   c. Who ultimately fulfills prophecies?

   d. Put it all together: How do all of these facts together corroborate everything you've already studied about the validity of God's Word?

7. From beginning to end, the Bible is full of fulfilled prophecies. Which ones support your Faith in God's Word the most? Explain

your answer. (Hint: If you don't know any prophecies, look in your Bible's concordance or try an online resource to help you gain familiarity with the hundreds of valid predictions the Bible makes.)

JESUS' VIEW OF SCRIPTURE

8. Here's a new idea for a bracelet to sell at bookstores and gas stations across the country: HDJUS? *How Did Jesus Use Scripture?* (Okay, maybe not.) Look up these gospel accounts and explain how Jesus' example helps you know how to use God's Word.

Matthew 4:1-11:

Mark 7:6-9:

Mark 12:24-27:

Luke 10:25-28:

9. Jesus gave a very specific reason for why He needed to die on the cross. What is that reason, and what does it say about Jesus' Faith in God's Word (Luke 24:25-27)?

10. How should we think about God's Word? Again, look at Jesus' example in the following verses and write down what you see.

    Matthew 5:17-18:

    John 17:17:

11. Looking back over questions 8 through 10, summarize Jesus' Faith in Scripture.

12. How does Jesus' example challenge and/or encourage you to put your complete Faith in God's Word? Or doesn't it? Explain your answer.

THE SUFFICIENCY OF SCRIPTURE

13. As you study God's Word, do you ever find yourself asking, *Why should I put my Faith in this Book?* Or maybe you know someone who doesn't believe in the Bible. Here are some verses that highlight some of the reasons God's Word should be important to your everyday life. *Pick two or three* verses below and summarize the main point of each in your own words. Which one do you find most relevant to your experiences?

Psalm 37:31:

Psalm 119:130:

John 15:3:

Acts 20:32:

James 1:21:

14. Next, read Isaiah 55:10-11. In this passage, God compared His Word to water that refreshes and nourishes the land.

   a. What are all of the ways that God's Word affects your Faith and your life in Him?

   b. Write down any new thoughts you have after reading this passage.

   c. Go back a few verses to Isaiah 55:8-9. Explain why this statement is or is not applicable to your Faith.

APPLYING THE BIBLE TO YOUR LIFE

15. How does David's statement in Psalm 119:59-60 relate to applying Scripture to your life today?

16. How did Jesus react to the people of His day who knew the Scripture but didn't have enough Faith to apply it to their lives?

   Luke 6:46:

   Luke 24:25:

17. King Josiah didn't have that problem. How did he go about making God's Word relevant to his life (2 Kings 23:2-4)?

18. What makes the Bible so unique? Muslims have the Koran. Hindus claim that the Vedas are divinely inspired. Mormons have *The Book of Mormon*. Zoroastrians have numerous ancient religious texts. How do you know that the Bible is what it claims to be? Look back over your answers to the questions in this chapter. Revisit some of the passages you looked up.

   a. State why you believe the Bible differs (or doesn't differ) from the sacred texts of all other religions.

b. Read 2 Timothy 3:16. What is one good reason we can trust the Bible over all other "sacred texts"?

19. God's Word can be tough to believe sometimes. It can be difficult to believe the strong claims it makes, especially the ones that fly in the face of modern culture. Paul addressed this in 1 Corinthians 1 and 2.

   a. How did Paul explain why some of God's statements are so difficult to believe (1 Corinthians 1:20-25)?

   b. So how do we begin to understand God's Word (1 Corinthians 2:9-11)?

20. Do you think you can love God and not love His Word? Why or why not?

21. If you are ready to start applying the teachings of the Bible to your everyday life, here's a good way to start:

- As you read the Bible, pray that God's Spirit will show you how it relates to specific areas of your life.
- Admit to yourself, honestly, what your life is like in this area.
- Make a plan for letting the Father be the boss in this area of your life.
- Implement practical steps to change. Find someone to talk to who will check your progress.

22. How do you think these four steps can help you apply God's Word to your life, if at all? Explain your answer.

SUMMARY

Come up with your own summary for this chapter. Be sure to answer this question in your conclusion: How important is God's Word to one's Faith?

CHAPTER 3

THE DIVINE NATURE

Hollywood and fiction writers love the nothing-is-as-it-seems motif. You've seen it before: the idea that there's some deep secret the protagonist must discover before he or she can discover the true meaning of life, that there's more than meets the eye. Movies and books lead us to discover hidden realities that profoundly affect our lives but lie just beneath our awareness. Well, guess what? There *is* more than meets the eye.

Jesus told us that "the kingdom of God is near" (Mark 1:15). Peter wrote about participating in the "divine nature" (2 Peter 1:4). What is all this talk about? Obviously God isn't the secretary-general of the UN, ruling His physical kingdom on earth. So what was Jesus talking about in His statement in the book of Mark? And what did Paul mean when he told his readers to focus "not on what is seen, but on what is unseen" (2 Corinthians 4:18) and that our battle is not against "flesh and blood" but something else, something not physical (Ephesians 6:12)?

Without sliding into new age, tripped-out philosophies, it's important for Christ-followers to understand that there are things going on that we can't see. That's why Faith is so crucial. If everything was plainly seen by the naked eye, Faith would be irrelevant. Instead, we live by the guidance of the Holy Spirit, participating in a divine realm that we scarcely understand. It's surreal. But it's true. Faith and God's Spirit will show you what it means.

THE HOLY SPIRIT

1. The book of Acts is full of instances where men and women who put their Faith in Christ witnessed the Holy Spirit's divine nature firsthand. Read Acts 13:1-3. Re-create the scene in your own words. What do you imagine it was like?

2. Give some indications from the following verses that the Holy Spirit is God. In one of your answers, state why it's important to put Faith in the Holy Spirit.

    Genesis 1:2:

    Psalm 139:7-8:

    Hebrews 9:14:

3. How is the Holy Spirit involved whenever people put their Faith in Christ?

   John 3:5-6:

   Ephesians 1:13-14:

   Titus 3:5:

4. Is this true in your life? Elaborate.

5. Go back to John, and this time look up John 16:7-15.

   a. What is God's Spirit up to today (verses 8-11)?

   b. How does He help you as a believer (verse 13)?

c. From this passage, what occupation would you say most closely defines the Spirit?

   a. Lawyer
   b. Teacher
   c. Press Secretary
   d. Counselor
   e. Other: _____

d. Explain your answer.

6. The Holy Spirit helps us reflect God's glory in our lives. Read Romans 8, one of the weightiest and most important chapters in the whole Bible. Record how the Spirit will help you live more like Christ.

Verse 2:

Verse 14:

Verse 16:

Verse 26:

7. Describe how the Holy Spirit played a role in Paul's missionary journeys and then draw some conclusions about how the Spirit works in your life.

Acts 16:6-7:

1 Corinthians 2:4:

SPIRITUAL GIFTS

Spiritual gifts are a major part of living out our Faith. We need to learn how to let the Spirit guide us to give glory to God with our talents and abilities. The Spirit is intricately tied to our gifts. Here's how...

8. God has given every person unique abilities to serve Him. The Spirit works in us to draw out these gifts, but we must first recognize them in ourselves and choose to use them for God's glory. Use 1 Corinthians 12 to help you answer the following questions.

a. Who has received spiritual gifts from the Holy Spirit (verses 7,11)?

b. Why are these gifts given (verse 7; see also 1 Peter 4:10)?

c. In what ways have you witnessed the "body of Christ" analogy? How do you think your gifts fit in (verses 12-20)?

d. Does God gift any two people in the same way? Why or why not (verses 28-30)?

9. What else can you learn about spiritual gifts from the Bible (Romans 12:6-8; Ephesians 4:11)?

Are you anxious to discover your spiritual gifts? God will reveal them to you as He "works in you to will and to act according to his good purpose" (Philippians 2:13). Remember, as a Christian you are supposed to have all the *fruit* of the Spirit, but you won't necessarily have all the *gifts* of the Spirit.

10. Maybe you already have an idea of how you are gifted spiritually. Hypothesize how you might be able to serve God with your abilities.

FELLOWSHIP

You've just seen how all believers in Christ make up one body. Obviously, there should be a real unity among believers; unfortunately, it doesn't always work out that way. Nevertheless, we are to do our part to promote a real united spirit among believers—to be there for one another and to encourage each other to keep our Faith in God. It's called fellowship. Worship and service with other believers can be a divine way that God works in our lives, families, and communities.

11. Read 1 John 3:1. If you are God's child and He is the Father of all Christ-followers, infer something about your relationship to other believers. If they are your "siblings," how should you think about and treat them?

12. The word *fellowship* is used to translate the Greek word *koinonia*, which means "sharing in common." God has given everyone much to

share. Look at the following verses and for each one write what you can share and one practical way to make it happen.

What to Share   **A Way to Share**

Galatians 6:2:

Galatians 6:6:

James 5:16:

1 John 4:11,21:

13. Imagine the following scenario: A few Christians go out for coffee, just shooting the breeze. They talk about class and sports and tell some jokes and funny stories. All in all, they have a pretty good time together. As one person leaves, he says, "Man, it's great to have good Christian fellowship!"

a. Is this real Christian fellowship?

b. Why or why not?

c. Is there really a right or wrong answer to this question? You decide.

14. In 1 Corinthians 12, you read that God sees all followers of Christ as part of one body, so we can be the Father's hands and feet in this world. If we—all who love and treasure Christ—make up just one body, what does that say about the necessity for fellowship, cooperation, and harmony?

15. Who is the head of this body? Why (Colossians 1:18)?

16. Ephesians 4:2-3 tells us how we can help preserve unity in this body. From this passage, what do you want to apply to your life, if anything?

17. Take a minute to reflect on your attitude toward other believers and your church. Is there someone who really bothers you? If so, write down what you can do to make the situation right.

18. Revisit Ephesians 4:11; this time read verses 12 and 13 as well.

   a. Specifically, what does this passage teach us about how Christ-followers should relate to one another?

   b. What happens to our Faith when believers are united as one body, helping each other Journey with God?

19. Stay in Ephesians and read 5:18-21.

   a. What do you think it means to be filled or even drunk with the Holy Spirit?

   b. Compare and contrast: What does being drunk on alcohol produce, and what does being drunk on the Spirit produce?

   c. Verses 19-21 list several results of being filled with the Spirit. Pick two or three and describe how you've experienced these results in your life, if you have.

20. Here are some other passages about being filled with the Spirit. What does each verse say, and how does it relate to your Faith, if at all?

   Acts 4:31:

Acts 11:24:

Romans 5:5:

21. Our Faith in the Spirit and His divine ways is not to be taken lightly. If we regularly ignore or show apathy to the Spirit's calling, we can find ourselves in danger of losing His guidance altogether. Read the following verses in parentheses and write a quick plan you can implement to avoid falling into either one of these Faith sinkholes (1 Thessalonians 5:19; Ephesians 4:30).

22. Stay in Ephesians 4:30 and look at the surrounding verses for context as you answer the questions that follow.

   a. What are some of the things that trouble God's Spirit?

b. Is there something in your life that grieves the Spirit?

c. If so, according to this passage, what do you need to do (verses 31-32)?

SUMMARY

Write your own summary of this chapter. Be sure to analyze how the Spirit, our gifts, and other believers play a role in our day-to-day living out the Faith. (Bonus points if you can show how all of these relate to the divine nature in 2 Peter 1:3-4.)

CHAPTER 4

THE ENEMY, THE KING, AND THE FATE OF BOTH

In World War II, the Germans invaded the Netherlands, among other countries. The languages of these two countries are similar enough that it was difficult to distinguish who was German and who was Dutch—a potentially life-threatening dilemma.

But the Dutch people found a way that they could distinguish themselves from their enemies: They could make the Germans say, "Schevenigen," the name of a coastal city in their country. The Germans couldn't say it without a distinct accent, so it became a sort of password for the Dutch to help them identify their enemies.

For Christ-followers, it's equally important to know our Enemy, not so we get intimidated or freaked out, but so we can distinguish him when we see him. Our Enemy is real and potent—more evil than Hitler, as you'll discover in this chapter. Satan wants to destroy Faith however possible. But it's equally, if not more, important to realize that his fate has already been decided. While battles continue to rage, Christ has won the war. We must have Faith in His assured return and victory.

1. Describe in your own words what Paul said in Ephesians 6:12 about our life in Christ. How have you experienced this battle?

2. Next, read 2 Timothy 2:3-4. How did Paul describe our Journey with God in this passage?

3. It can be strange to think about, but our Faith leads us into hand-to-hand combat (continuing Paul's analogy) with our Enemy. Read Revelation 12:9-10.

   a. Who is the Enemy?

   b. What happened to him?

4. One of our Enemy's primary objectives is to undermine our Faith and our love of Jesus Christ. His tactic is to twist the truth and try to deceive us into compromising our Faith. What do you notice about Satan, the "god of this age," from the following verses?

   Luke 8:12:

   John 8:44:

2 Corinthians 4:3-4:

2 Corinthians 11:3:

2 Corinthians 11:14:

5. Synthesize all of these descriptions of Satan. How can you prepare yourself for his attacks?

6. If that wasn't enough, Peter also painted a portrait of the Enemy in 1 Peter 5:8-9. Write it out in your own words.

7. Peter knew what Satan is like. Just before He died, Jesus warned Peter about the Enemy of his Faith.

   a. What bombshell news item did Jesus drop on Peter in Luke 22:31?

   b. Even more important, perhaps, do you think Satan is asking these questions about you? Why or why not?

8. To paraphrase James 4:4, when we go against our Faith and break God's law, we sin and side with our Enemy. Read this verse and state some ways that you have been too friendly with your Enemy. Then list some ways that you want to align yourself more fully with the Father and His ways.

9. You've studied how horrible and powerful the Enemy is. But because of Christ's work on our behalf, the story doesn't end there. Skip down a

few verses to James 4:7-10. Answer this two-part question: How can we get Satan out of our lives, and how can we make sure we stay close to God?

> Some say, "I have my faults, but at the bottom, I have a good heart." Alas! It is this that deceives you, for your heart is the worst part of you.
> —CHARLES H. SPURGEON*

THE ASSURANCE OF VICTORY

10. We used to be slaves to evil, that is, to Satan. We couldn't help but sin. But that was before Christ saved us from that slavery. Read about our emancipation in Hebrews 2:14-15. Have you ever considered the fact that you are now set free from the power of evil in your life? Think about it for a second or two and jot down some of your thoughts. Do you feel free? If so, in what ways?

---

*Taken from *Foundations for Faith* (Colorado Springs, Colo.: NavPress, 1980), p. 34.

11. First John 4:4 and Revelation 12:11 speak to this newfound freedom and victory over evil. From these two verses, make a couple of observations about battling the Enemy of your Faith.

12. The day-to-day living of your Faith really is a battle between good and evil. We must wage war on our sins to walk boldly with the Father. We also must have a strong defense against the surprise attacks of our Enemy who would like nothing more than to "sift us like wheat." Read about your defensive gear in Ephesians 6:14-18. What practical steps can you take to implement all of this gear in your everyday life?

Equipment   **Practical Steps**

13. Because we are free from the grip of evil in our lives, we are able to fight the Devil's plan, not only in our own lives, but also in the world around us. Read Romans 8:37-39. How might this passage bolster your Faith to take on the Enemy?

CHRIST'S RETURN

14. Read Jesus' promise to His followers in John 14:2-4. List the three parts of His promise and explain why this promise is central to the Faith.

15. John 14 isn't the only place Christ addressed this issue. Read the following verses. What did Jesus say about His return to earth?

Matthew 16:27:

Matthew 24:27:

Mark 13:26-27:

Luke 12:40:

16. We've heard from Jesus Himself. But what did others say about Christ's return? How does each of these verses corroborate what He said?

Acts 1:9-11:

1 Thessalonians 2:19:

1 Thessalonians 5:2-6:

17. Before Jesus comes back, however, certain things must transpire. Use Matthew 24 to answer the following questions.

   a. What sorts of things will happen as the time of Christ's return grows near (verses 6-7)?

   b. What will true believers do during this time (verses 13-14)?

   c. What else will clue the people in that something big is about to happen (verse 29)?

   d. There will be clues and signs, but no one knows for sure when Christ will return except whom (verse 36)?

18. With the popularity of apocalyptic movies and books such as the Left Behind series, people these days seem fairly hyped up about Christ's possible return. Read what Jesus said in Matthew 24:42-44. What sort of attitude was He calling us to possess?

19. According to these verses, how should we act?

   a. Obsessed with Christ's return
   b. Indifferent
   c. Scared
   d. Level-headed and ready

20. Explain your answer.

THE GRAND FINALE

Many good people have just as many ways of interpreting the Bible's teaching about Christ's return. Some say there will be a Rapture in which all believers will meet up in the sky before the Tribulation, the rule of the Antichrist. Some say Christians will live through the time of the Antichrist. Some believe all the supposed end-times events have already taken place. Suffice it to say that while there are some clues about these events in the Bible, ultimately the most important thing to remember is that Christ *is* coming back. When and how He returns is not as important as being ready.

21. Read 1 Thessalonians 4:13-18.

   a. What are we supposed to do with this knowledge (verse 18)?

   b. React personally: How does the knowledge of Christ's eventual return make a difference in your day-to-day life?

22. According to the Bible, how should a follower of Christ feel about Christ's return? Read the following verses and fuse their main points: 2 Timothy 4:8, James 5:7-8, and 1 Peter 1:13.

23. Compare 2 Peter 3:10-13 and 1 John 3:2-3. In a short paragraph, explain how Christ's return should affect your ultimate Faith in Him.

24. Christ isn't waiting to return just to keep everyone in eager expectation. He waits out of grace, love, and a joy in the glory of God.

   a. Even more specifically than the reason given above, why do you think Christ is waiting to return?

   b. Now see what the Bible says about this issue. How does it resemble or differ from your answer (Matthew 24:14; 2 Peter 3:9)?

25. Read Revelation 20:10 and 21:5-7. How does Satan's final outcome contrast with Christ's fate?

SUMMARY

Write a summary of this chapter. Here's one topic to address: Why is it important to remember Christ's return as we battle our Enemy?

www.ingramcontent.com/pod-product-compliance
Lightning Source LLC
Chambersburg PA
CBHW071223070526
44584CB00019B/3131